Animal Antics

TIGERS

Copyright © ticktock Entertainment Ltd 2007
First published in Great Britain in 2007 by ticktock Media Ltd.,
Unit 2, Orchard Business Centre, North Farm Road,
Tunbridge Wells, Kent, TN2 3XF

Author: Monica Hughes
Designers: Alix Wood and Emma Randall
Editor: Rebecca Clunes

ISBN 978 1 84696 497 8 pbk

Printed in China

This is Stanley.
He likes animals.
He would like to
be an animal.

Stanley's toys

THIS WAY UP

Which animal would YOU like to be?

Stanley would like to be

a shark

an ant

a caterpillar

a bat

and a snail.

Most of all
Stanley would
like to be a
tiger.

Stanley
loves tigers.

Stanley knows a lot about tigers.
He knows tigers are the
biggest of all cats.

They are very **rare**.
Most tigers live alone.
They can live for 15-20 years
in the wild.

True or False?
Tigers can live up to 25 years in a zoo.

Answers for True or False are on page 32.

Did You Know?

Rare white tigers have white fur, black stripes and blue eyes.

Most tigers have orange fur with brown stripes.

They hide in long grass and deep **jungle.**

Their coats give them good **camouflage**.

True or False?
Tiger cubs have the same pattern of stripes as their mother.

incisor

canine

10

Adult tigers
have 30 teeth.

Their teeth are so strong they
can bite through bone.

They have small sharp
incisors at the front.

They have long pointed
canines at the side.

Did You Know?
A tiger's roar can
be heard from
10 kilometres away.

Stanley has a pet cat.

He likes her but thinks
a tiger would be a
better pet.

True or False?
Cats were treated as
gods in Ancient Egypt.

Do **YOU** think a tiger would make a good pet for Stanley?

feeds his cat
every morning and evening.

She eats tinned or dried cat food.

She also likes fresh chicken and fish.
What would Stanley feed a tiger?

CATFOOD

True or False?
Cats eat grass.

Too much milk can make a cat sick.

Tigers stalk their **prey**.

They often wait
at **waterholes**.

True or False?
Tigers eat fish.

Tigers creep closer and closer and then leap.

They kill their prey with a bite to the neck or throat.

Did You Know?
Tigers can jump up to nine metres in the air.

17

Stanley thinks his cat is a lot like a tiger.

They both have sharp claws.

They both lick themselves
to keep themselves
clean.

They can both see well in the dark.

Did You Know?
Some tiger claws are
10 centimetres long.

Stanley knows that tigers and cats both have long whiskers.

Their whiskers help them feel how close things are.

Did You Know?
The Manx cat does not have a tail.

Tigers and cats both have long tails.

They swish their tails when they are angry.

Stanley knows that tigers live near lakes and rivers.

Stanley's cat does NOT like water.

Tigers like to lie in the water to keep cool. They are very good at swimming.

Stanley's cat is afraid of dogs.

She climbs a tree
if she sees a dog.

Stanley thinks a tiger would never be afraid.

When Stanley's cat had kittens she was a good mother.

If she needed to move the kittens, she carried them gently in her mouth.

Stanley is afraid a tiger would carry him.

Did You Know?

Tiger cubs stay with their mother for two years.

Do YOU think
a tiger would
do that?

Stanley loves his pet cat.

He likes to play with her
and to hug her.

He likes it when
she **purrs**.

Stanley thinks she is
a good pet for him.

Did You Know?

Cats came to Britain 1000 years ago.

Stanley still likes tigers.

But he knows a tiger would not be a good pet.

A tiger is too **big** for a cat-flap!

Glossary

Camouflage   Markings that make an animal difficult to see.

Jungle   Forest with lots of trees and plants.

Prey   An animal that is hunted for food.

Purrs   The noise a cat makes when it is happy.

Rare   Not often seen.

Waterhole   A pool of water.

True or False answers

Page 7   True

Page 9   False
All tigers have a
different pattern
of stripes.

Page 12   True

Page 14   True

Page 17   True